# Willa

The Story of
**Willa Cather,**
an American Writer

AMY EHRLICH
Illustrated by WENDELL MINOR

A PAULA WISEMAN BOOK
**SIMON & SCHUSTER BOOKS FOR YOUNG READERS**
NEW YORK LONDON TORONTO SYDNEY NEW DELHI

SIMON & SCHUSTER BOOKS FOR YOUNG READERS
An imprint of Simon & Schuster Children's Publishing Division
1230 Avenue of the Americas, New York, New York 10020
Text copyright © 2016 by Amy Ehrlich • Illustrations copyright © 2016 by Wendell Minor
SIMON & SCHUSTER BOOKS FOR YOUNG READERS is a trademark of Simon & Schuster, Inc.
For information about special discounts for bulk purchases, please contact
Simon & Schuster Special Sales at 1-866-506-1949 or business@simonandschuster.com.
The Simon & Schuster Speakers Bureau can bring authors to your live event.
For more information or to book an event, contact the Simon & Schuster Speakers Bureau
at 1-866-248-3049 or visit our website at www.simonspeakers.com.
Book design by Laurent Linn
The text for this book is set in Minister Std.
The illustrations for this book are rendered in watercolor and gouache.
Manufactured in China
0716 SCP
First Edition
2  4  6  8  10  9  7  5  3  1
Library of Congress Cataloging-in-Publication Data
Ehrlich, Amy, 1942– author.
Willa : the Story of Willa Cather, an American Writer / Amy Ehrlich ; illustrated by Wendell Minor.
pages cm
Summary: "A chapter book biography of Willa Cather, an American novelist"—Provided by publisher.
"A Paula Wiseman Book"
ISBN 978-0-689-86573-2 (hardback)
ISBN 978-1-4424-9870-9 (eBook)
1. Cather, Willa, 1873–1947—Juvenile literature. 2. Novelists, American—20th century—Biography—
Juvenile literature. I. Minor, Wendell, illustrator. II. Title.
PS3505.A87Z634 2016
813'.52—dc23
[B]
2014027586

With gratitude for the help Doug and
Charlene Hoschouer gave me in Red Cloud,
and to Alan Boye for talking to me about Nebraska.

—A. E.


The artist wishes to thank the Willa Cather Foundation
and the University of Nebraska and the Willa Cather
Archive as reference sources in creating his watercolor
paintings and drawings in this book.

—W. M.

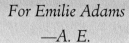

*For Emilie Adams*
*—A. E.*

*To the timeless voice of Willa Cather,*
*and to the young reader who will listen*

*—W. M.*

# Willow Shade (1874–1883)

Ever since she could remember, Willa lived with her family in Willow Shade, a house as pretty as its name. It was made of brick and had a white portico in front with four columns. This was in Virginia, in Winchester County near a town called Back Creek. In the family were Willa's parents and Grandma Boak and four children, Willa (first), then Roscoe, Douglass, and Jessica.

Willa's parents gave her the freedom to do what she wanted and become whoever she would be. Grandma Boak helped with Willa's education, reading books to her before she started school. Some were children's books, but Grandma Boak also read Willa long passages from the family Bible, and these echoed in her thoughts.

In good weather Willa played outdoors with Roscoe and her father's sheepdog, Vic. Sometimes Marjie, the hired girl, came too. They went down the double S road and explored the leafy woods, where dogwood and wild laurel bloomed. Her father taught Willa to set traps for rabbits and took her with him on horseback when he went to bring the sheep to the fold.

The Civil War was hardly over. Willa liked to think she'd been named for her mother's brother William who'd been killed at Manassas, fighting for the Confederacy. Their part of Virginia was close to the Northern Union states, and her parents had been divided—her father's family were Unionists and her mother's were Confederates.

Willa's parents never owned slaves but her grandparents did. Before the War her grandmother helped a young slave named Nancy Till escape, taking her across the Potomac River, where agents of the Underground Railroad were waiting to bring her to Canada. Twenty-five years later Nancy came home again to see her mother. This woman was called Aunt Till, and Willa was in the upstairs bedroom when they met, watching as they fell into each other's arms.

So many people came to Willow Shade! Friends and relatives from Winchester and Baltimore came, and the tin peddler, and Uncle Billy Parks the broom maker. Freed slaves worked in the fields and house, and countrywomen from Timber Ridge and North Mountain helped with preserving and candle making and piecing quilts. During the winter evenings the servants sat around the great fireplace in the kitchen cracking nuts and telling stories. They were Willa's friends and she was allowed to stay and listen.

Trees, rocks, creeks, hills. The animals in the woods. A farm in its seasons. A meeting between a mother and daughter. Willa's life was interesting every single day. She never imagined it would change.

# Going West (1883)

In the West, beyond the settled hills of Virginia, there was a vast open land. People said a man could plow a furrow in rich dirt all the way to the horizon. The railroads were crossing this open land on their way to the Pacific.

Willa's aunt and uncle and her Cather grandparents went West to Nebraska. They lived on the prairie in a place they named after themselves: Catherton. In Virginia, after Willa's father's sheep barn burned down and her two aunts became sick from a lung disease called tuberculosis, Willa's father decided to sell Willow Shade and all they owned. They were going West too.

By April they were ready. The family started to board the train at Back Creek. Then their sheepdog, Vic, who'd been given to a neighbor, escaped and came running across the fields, dragging his chain. He did not want them to go West and Willa didn't either.

At the Burlington and Missouri depot outside the prairie town of Red Cloud, Nebraska, Uncle George's wagons were waiting to bring them to Catherton. There were no hills, no fields, no fences. Just red prairie grass and wind. The road was nothing, just a faint trail in the grass.

Willa sat in the hay in the jolting wagon and tried hard not to cry. Her father said you had to show grit in a new land. But as they drove farther and farther into the countryside, it was as if her personality and the world she had known were being erased, as if she'd come to the end of everything.

## On the Divide (1883–1884)

Grandfather Cather's homestead was on a high rolling plain between the Republican River and the Little Blue. Prairie dogs lived in prairie dog towns and big rattlesnakes slid through the grass. On the farm the Cathers had only canned food to eat and nobody paid any attention to Willa. At first she thought she would die of homesickness.

Her mother was often ill and her brothers were busy planting corn. But Willa had a pony and all the freedom she could want. That first

summer on the Divide she rode around the countryside from morning to night, following the pioneers' wagon tracks where sunflowers grew in a golden ribbon.

She liked to go on errands and get the mail at the post office three miles away. There was a school district in Catherton and classes were held

in a one-room wooden schoolhouse. Willa went for three months in the winter, bringing her dinner and riding her pony over the frozen ground.

The Cathers' closest neighbors were the

Lambrechts, who'd come to Nebraska from Germany. There were many foreign families on the Divide—Germans, Scandinavians, French, Bohemians, and Russians. America beckoned to them, promising a better life. But when the immigrants arrived with their tin trunks and their oilcloth bundles, and their children and babies held close, they had to work like mules.

Men who had been cigar makers in the old country drove the plow, breaking up the rough sod for planting and building. The women endured the dirt sifting down from the walls and ceilings of their sod dugouts, and tried to keep order in this strange place.

Willa played with the foreign children, but most of all she loved talking to the women as they did the baking or made dinner for their families. She had dozens of questions, and in their broken English, the women patiently answered them. Perhaps they understood that Willa was lonely too.

The immigrant women's stories about the old country were vivid and thrilling to Willa. Listening to them it was as if she'd actually gotten inside another person's skin. As she rode across the prairie, Willa thought that no other adventure had ever carried her so far.

# Red Cloud (1884–1890)

Willa's father tried farming on the prairie but decided to sell real estate instead. He opened up an office in the county seat of Red Cloud, named after a chief of the Oglala Sioux tribe.

Red Cloud was an exciting place to be. It had a business street with redbrick buildings and a roundhouse. Eight trains a day passed through it, coming and going between Chicago, Kansas City, and Denver. There was a new Red Cloud Opera House, and Willa and her friends loved to go to the train depot to watch actors from the touring companies arrive in town.

The Cathers rented a little house on the corner of Third and Cedar. The children slept in a row in the attic. Every morning Willa ran outside to play with the Miner girls, who lived next door. The girls liked to put on shows in the

Miners' parlor, with Willa writing and directing and acting the men's parts.

Dressing up gave Willa a chance to try on other lives, and when she was fourteen she cut her hair short and started calling herself William Cather Jr. or sometimes William Cather, M.D.

Willa thought she might be a doctor when she grew up, like her friends Dr. McKeeby and Dr. Damerell. A lot of Willa's friends in Red Cloud were adults. Adults were more interesting than children and they talked to Willa in a serious and cultured way.

But many people in town thought Willa Cather was a show-off. What did she mean dressing up like a boy and teaching herself anatomy by dissecting frogs and toads in her basement? Would she go on to cats and dogs next?

For all her boldness, this kind of talk hurt Willa. Her external self had nothing to do with the way she felt inside. Her mother had made Willa a room in the attic, and Willa furnished it with a desk and washstand, and hung rose-patterned wallpaper. She loved to go up there, to read and be alone.

Adventure stories like *Treasure Island, The Three Musketeers,* and *The Adventures of Huckleberry Finn,* then novels like *Madame*

*Bovary* and *Anna Karenina* were like opening a window for Willa. They helped her escape the town's narrow expectations about what a girl could and could not do.

# Lincoln (1890–1895)

The world was waiting—it was calling to Willa. When she was sixteen she was excited to go to college in the state capital of Lincoln. It had paved streets and horsecars and gaslights, and a skyscraper six stories high.

Willa still meant to be a doctor and she studied hard. But in her first year at college she wrote an essay on a Scottish writer named Thomas Carlyle that was so good, her professor had it printed in the newspaper. That Sunday when Willa opened the *Nebraska State Journal*, she saw her name in print for the first time. She'd always lived in her imagination, but now Willa realized she could be a writer.

She started out writing about plays and musicals that she saw. Night after night Willa was in the audience at the Lansing or Funke, the two theaters in Lincoln. Then she went to the *Journal* office and wrote her newspaper column that was called "One Way of Putting It." She was paid $1.00 and she needed the money.

Banks were failing all over the country and crops were failing. In Nebraska a hot wind burned up the corn in three days. There were two more children in Willa's family—six all together now—and her father could no longer support her.

Willa knew she could earn a living. Her column was controversial and strong-minded. People were talking about it all over the Midwest. Then she was asked to teach at the Nebraska Chautauqua, a summer assembly where thousands of Nebraskans stayed in tents near the Big Blue River and went to lectures and concerts. Willa was proud to be among the scholars and musicians who came from as far away as Chicago.

After college it was almost unbearable to have to go back to Red Cloud where nothing important had ever happened and nothing ever would. Willa loved her family but felt far from them for the first time, trapped in the middle of nowhere. Her triumphs as a journalist and at the Nebraska Chautauqua might have been a dream.

# Back East (1896–1911)

Willa planned to write her own stories and novels, but she also needed to support herself. Her first full-time job was at *Home Monthly*, a women's magazine about doing housework and making pies and raising babies. Willa thought it was namby-pamby, but the offices were back east in Pittsburgh, only a hundred miles from where she was born.

At first Willa lived in cheap boardinghouses, then she met a new friend named Isabelle McClung and moved in with Isabelle's family on Murray Hill Avenue in the fancy Squirrel Hill section of town. Willa had her own room and study on the third floor and could write and write, all night long if she wanted to.

She was making good progress and several of her stories were published in national magazines like *Cosmopolitan* and *Saturday Evening Post*. But then S. S. McClure, the publisher of *McClure's Magazine,* learned about Willa and hired her as his associate editor.

*McClure's* was in New York City and it seemed that Willa had at last found the worldly success she wanted. She lived in a studio apartment in Greenwich Village, a neighborhood of artists and poets. She could go to the opera every week and to museums and the theater. *McClure's* was a busy and thrilling enterprise, and her job there was very important.

But time was passing, and Willa's strength was going into work that was not her own. S. S. McClure knew she was restless and offered her an exciting assignment—to move to Boston and write about Mary Baker Eddy, the founder of the Christian Science Church.

It was in Boston on Charles Street in a long drawing room filled with beautiful paintings and a bright fire burning that Willa met an older writer named Sarah Orne Jewett. Miss Jewett

understood Willa immediately. She wrote Willa
a letter warning her that she needed to leave
the magazine and find her own quiet center.
Only then would Willa realize the true nature
of her talent.

# Coming Home (1912–1938)

Willa had been to Europe many times. With her friend Edith Lewis, she had traveled by train and steamboat through England and Italy and France. Europe was the Old World, the birthplace of literature and art, and several of Willa's early stories were set there.

But she was thinking of a new kind of story, one that came not from her admiration of other places and writers but from her own experience. When Willa finally left *McClure's* she wrote "The Bohemian Girl" and "Alexandra," stories about the immigrant families she had known in Nebraska. They came to her so easily. Willa was finding the path she wanted to travel and it led back to her childhood.

Outside Red Cloud on the Republican River was a sandbar with a stand of cottonwood trees where Willa and her brothers used to go. It was

called Far Island. They built campfires on the
beach and told stories and watched the flicker-
ing stars. Sometimes they imagined themselves
in Indian country in the Southwest desert.
What adventures they would have!

And now her brother Douglass was working
for the Santa Fe Railroad and living in Winslow,
Arizona. After her hard years at *McClure's*, Willa
decided to visit him. The vast new landscape of
canyons and cliff dwellings and red stone hills

carved from the earth calmed Willa, reminding her of that first summer on the Divide.

In July and August on her way back East, she stayed with her family in Red Cloud. Everything was much as she had left it. But this time instead of feeling there was nothing for her, Willa was overwhelmed by the beauty of the prairie. She wanted to see her old friends but no one else. She wanted to lose herself in the expanse and silence of that place and describe what she felt.

From then on Willa would write more simply and naturally, as if her feet were finding the road home on a dark night. As she worked, she got to deeper levels of feeling and remembered more and more. Her final novel, *Sapphira and the Slave Girl*, is set back in Virginia, in Willow Shade at the end of the Civil War. In the last chapter a little girl sits in an upstairs bedroom, watching as a mother and daughter meet again, falling into each other's arms.

## An American Writer

Willa became famous. Her books sold hundreds of thousands of copies and won many awards, including the Pulitzer Prize. The stories she told about the hopes and tragedies of immigrants living on the prairie struck readers and critics as utterly fresh and new. No American writer had ever written about this land before or seen its people as heroes.

Willa's life journey from Virginia to Nebraska to the cities of the East Coast is itself an

American story of possibility and striving, self-invention and achievement. As a writer, Willa turned her own life into material for her art. She wrote poetry, essays, and short stories, but is best known for her novels. Some of them like *O Pioneers!*, *My Antonia*, and *Death Comes for the Archbishop* are American classics. These books continue to be discovered by new generations of readers and have influenced other writers to this day.

Willa died in 1947 at the age of seventy-three. On her gravestone is a quote from *My Antonia*: ". . . that is happiness, to be dissolved into something complete and great."

"For the first time perhaps since that land emerged from the waters of geologic ages, a human face was set toward it with love and yearning. . . . Her eyes drank in the breadth of it, until her tears blinded her. . . . The history of every country begins in the heart of a man or woman."

—FROM O PIONEERS!

**1873**

Willa was born on December 7 in Back Creek Valley, Virginia, near the Blue Ridge Mountains. She was named Wilella but called Willie by her family and friends. Willa was a name she made up for herself.

**1874**

The family moved to Willa's grandfather Cather's sheep farm. Her grandmother Rachel Boak came to live with them. She read the Bible to Willa and showed her how to write her letters. She was Willa's first teacher.

**1877**

Willa's grandparents left Virginia for Webster County, Nebraska, where their son Charles and his wife Frances lived. Willa's oldest brother, Roscoe, was born. She later had three more brothers—Douglass, James, and John—and two sisters, Jessica and Elsie. Willa was closer to her brothers than her sisters, especially Roscoe and Douglass, who were next to her in age.

**1883**

Willa and her family—including Grandmother Boak, the hired girl Marjorie Anderson and her brother, and two cousins—moved to Nebraska to join her Cather relatives. Willa went to a one-room school and was influenced by the stories of the European immigrant women who lived on the prairie.

## 1884

Willa's family moved to Red Cloud, a town sixteen miles away. William Ducker, an English storekeeper, taught Willa Latin and Greek, and the Weiners, a European Jewish couple, lent her books from their library and Mrs. Weiner read to her in French and German.

## 1890

At sixteen Willa graduated from high school in Red Cloud, one in a class of three. She wanted to go to the University of Nebraska, but first had to go to a preparatory school in Lincoln.

## 1891

Willa wrote an essay "Concerning Thos. Carlyle," signing it only "W. C." Her English teacher submitted it to the *Nebraska State Journal*. It was Willa's first published writing and it changed her ambitions from medicine to literature. She met Dorothy Canfield Fisher.

## 1892

Willa became editor of the university's student journal. Her short story "Peter" was published in *The Mahogany Tree*, a Boston literary magazine.

## 1895

Willa graduated from the University of Nebraska. She wrote as a journalist for two local papers. Her special interests were music and theater. On a visit to Chicago, Willa saw the Metropolitan Opera. In Lincoln she met Stephen Crane.

## 1896

Willa's story "On the Divide" was published in the *Overland Monthly*, with a national distribution. She went to Pittsburgh to work for the women's magazine *Home Monthly*. The following year and many years afterward Willa returned to Red Cloud for visits, staying in touch with her family and friends.

## 1899

Willa met Isabelle McClung, the daughter of a Pittsburgh judge. They developed a deep friendship and Willa moved in with Isabelle's family.

## 1903

Willa's first book, a poetry collection called *April Twilights*, was published. She met Edith Lewis, who grew up in Lincoln and became her lifelong companion.

## 1905

*The Troll Garden*, a short story collection, was published. Willa met Mark Twain.

## 1906

Willa became managing editor at *McClure's* magazine. She moved to New York City and lived in Greenwich Village.

## 1908

Willa met Sarah Orne Jewett, a Maine writer who became an important mentor.

## 1912

Willa's first novel, *Alexander's Bridge*, was published. Willa visited her brother Douglass in Arizona.

## 1913

*O Pioneers!*, Willa's first novel set on the prairie, was published. It was followed by two others, *The Song of the Lark* and *My Antonia*. These books are sometimes called her prairie trilogy.

## 1915

*The Song of the Lark* was published. It joined Willa's memories of the prairie to her interest in music. Part of the novel took place in the Southwest.

## 1918

*My Antonia* was published. The heroine, Antonia Shimerda, was based on memories of Annie Pavelka, a childhood friend. Many readers regard it as Willa's masterpiece. H. L. Mencken, a famous critic, wrote, "No romantic novel written in America, by man or woman, is one half so beautiful as *My Antonia*."

## 1920

With Edith Lewis, Willa went to Europe. In France she visited the grave of a G. P. Cather, a cousin who was killed in World War I.

## 1922

*One of Ours*, based on G. P. Cather's story and his letters home, was published.

## 1923

Willa received the Pulitzer Prize for Fiction for *One of Ours*. *A Lost Lady*, based on memories of the wife of a banker in Red Cloud, was published.

## 1924

Willa met D. H. Lawrence.

### 1925
Willa met Robert Frost. *The Professor's House* was published. Willa and Edith Lewis went to the Southwest.

### 1926
*My Mortal Enemy* was published.

### 1927
*Death Comes for the Archbishop*, based on a biography of a missionary in the Southwest, was published. Reviewers praised it as an American classic and a great work of literature.

### 1928
Willa's father died and her mother had a stroke. Willa returned to Red Cloud for a month. She traveled to Quebec City with Edith Lewis.

### 1930
Willa met the violinist Yehudi Menuhin and his family.

### 1931
Willa's mother died in California. Willa visited Red Cloud for the last time. *Shadows on the Rock*, set in Quebec City, was published.

### 1932
*Obscure Destinies* was published. It was Willa's final collection of short stories.

### 1933
Willa began work on *Lucy Gayheart*, set like *The Song of the Lark* in a town based on Red Cloud.

### 1936
*Not Under Forty*, a collection of Willa's essays on literature, was published.

**1938**

Willa's brother Douglass and her friend Isabelle McClung died.

**1940**

Willa's last novel *Sapphira and the Slave Girl*, set in her childhood home in Virginia, was published. She met Norwegian novelist Sigrid Undset.

**1942**

Willa met Truman Capote.

**1945**

Willa's brother Roscoe died.

**1947**

Willa died on April 24. She was buried in the White Mountains, in Jaffrey, New Hampshire.

There are always more men than women on lists of major American writers. This reflects the circumstances of women's lives in the nineteenth and early twentieth centuries rather than the quality of their work. At that time writing was not considered an appropriate career for women. It was so difficult for American women to receive serious recognition as writers that many of them took men's names as pseudonyms or used initials to disguise their true identities.

But during the past fifty years, in the era of modern feminism, many important women writers have been discovered, rediscovered, or widely published for the first time. Here are some who were Willa's contemporaries, along with mention of their works and the conditions of their lives.

### Harriet Beecher Stowe (1811–1896)

Harriet Beecher Stowe was an abolitionist whose great antislavery novel *Uncle Tom's Cabin* (1852) was the most widely read novel of its time. Many people, perhaps including Abraham Lincoln, credited her with helping to start the Civil War. She campaigned for women's rights, comparing the condition of a married woman to that of a slave.

## Julia Ward Howe (1819–1910)

Remembered today as the author of *Battle Hymn of the Republic*, Julia Ward Howe wrote intense and highly personal poetry. Her collection *Passion-Flowers* was published anonymously but her identity was soon discovered. Her repressive husband was so shocked by the book that he isolated her in the country and threatened to take custody of their children.

## Emily Dickinson (1830–1886)

Considered one of America's greatest poets, Emily Dickinson lived as a recluse in her family home in Amherst, Massachusetts. Though she wrote more than 1,800 poems, fewer than a dozen were published in her lifetime. Her poetry broke all the conventions of the era, both in its structure and its sense of desolation.

## Louisa May Alcott (1832–1888)

Louisa May Alcott, best known as the author of *Little Women*, worked as a writer to help support her family. She spent part of her childhood in a utopian community and was an abolitionist and nurse during the Civil War. Late in her life she took the pen name A. M. Barnard to avoid being identified as a woman.

## Sarah Orne Jewett (1849–1909)

Born on the Maine coast, Sarah Orne Jewett was best known for her regional novel *The Country of the Pointed Firs* and her short story "A White Heron." Her writing style was descriptive and precise. She was influenced by Harriet Beecher Stowe and was in turn an important influence on Willa Cather.

### Kate Chopin (1851–1904)

The first woman writer to deal realistically with romantic relationships, Kate Chopin was not accepted in her own time. Willa Cather reviewed her work in the *Pittsburgh Leader* and criticized its "trite and sordid theme." In the 1960s Chopin's novel *The Awakening* was revived and she is now considered a vital literary precursor of modern women writers.

### Charlotte Perkins Gilman (1860–1935)

Charlotte Perkins Gilman is the author of *The Yellow Wallpaper*. She based this story of a woman who has a mental breakdown after her child was born on her own experience. A committed feminist, when she separated from her husband she traveled around the country giving speeches about women's rights and social reform.

### Edith Wharton (1862–1937)

Along with Willa Cather, Edith Wharton is regarded as the greatest American woman writer of the early twentieth century. She won the Pulitzer Prize in 1921 for *The Age of Innocence*. Her other important novels include *The House of Mirth* and *Ethan Frome*. She came from an upper-class background and scorned American culture.

### Gertrude Stein (1874–1946)

Considered by many to be a genius, from an early age Gertrude Stein did what she wanted. She collected modern art, lived in Paris with her life partner Alice B. Toklas, and wrote in a disjointed style that few could understand. Her best-known books are *Three Lives* and *The Autobiography of Alice B. Toklas*.

## Dorothy Canfield Fisher (1879–1958)

A social activist and educator who established the Montessori childcare system in the United States, Dorothy Canfield Fisher wrote twenty-two novels—including several for children—and eighteen works of nonfiction. She and Willa Cather were friends for more than fifty years.

## Dorothy Parker (1893–1967)

Dorothy Parker had a hard and unhappy life. She was an activist who supported civil liberties. In New York she worked for *Vogue* and *Vanity Fair*. Later she moved to Hollywood and wrote for the movies, receiving an Academy Award nomination for the screenplay of *A Star Is Born*. She was famous for her dark wit and sense of irony.

## Katherine Anne Porter (1890–1980)

Best known for her novel *Ship of Fools* and her novella *Pale Horse, Pale Rider*, Katherine Anne Porter had a difficult childhood. She married at sixteen and worked as a journalist. In the 1920s she became involved with the Mexican revolutionary movement. She won a Pulitzer Prize in 1966 for her short stories.

## Zora Neale Hurston (1891–1960)

Raised in the all-black town of Eatonville, Florida, Zora Neale Hurston became involved in the Harlem Renaissance in New York City. In addition to writing fiction, she was a cultural anthropologist and collected folklore from the American South and the Caribbean. Her novel *Their Eyes Were Watching God* is considered a masterpiece of African-American literature.

### Edna St. Vincent Millay (1892–1950)

Famous for her poetry, Edna St. Vincent Millay was also a feminist and a journalist. She grew up in poverty with a single mother and learned to think for herself at an early age. She won her first poetry prize at fourteen and began to publish her poems a year later. In 1923 she became the third woman to win a Pulitzer Prize for poetry.

### Margaret Mitchell (1900–1949)

Margaret Mitchell was the author of *Gone with the Wind*, for which she won both the National Book Award and the Pulitzer Prize. The novel took ten years to write and portrays the Civil War and Reconstruction from a Southern point of view. It has sold more than 30 million copies throughout the world.

# BIBLIOGRAPHY

**Books by Willa Cather**

*O Pioneers!* Boston: Houghton Mifflin Company, 1913.

*The Song of the Lark.* Boston: Houghton Mifflin Company, 1915.

*My Antonia.* Boston: Houghton Mifflin Company, 1918.

*A Lost Lady.* New York: Alfred A. Knopf, 1923.

*The Professor's House.* New York: Alfred A. Knopf, 1925.

*Death Comes for the Archbishop.* New York: Alfred A. Knopf, 1927.

*Shadows on the Rock.* New York: Alfred A. Knopf, 1931.

*Sapphira and the Slave Girl.* New York: Alfred A. Knopf, 1940.

**Books about Willa Cather**

Bennett, Mildred R. *The World of Willa Cather.* Lincoln: University of Nebraska Press, 1951.

Lewis, Edith. *Willa Cather Living: A Personal Record.* New York: Alfred A. Knopf, 1953.

O'Brien, Sharon. *Willa Cather: The Emerging Voice.* Cambridge: Harvard University Press, 1997.

Woodress, James. *Willa Cather: A Literary Life.* Lincoln: University of Nebraska Press, 1987.

## Other Sources

O'Brien, Sharon. Chronology. *Cather: Later Novels.* New York: Library of America, 1990.

Showalter, Elaine. *A Jury of Her Peers: Celebrating American Women Writers from Anne Bradstreet to Annie Proulx.* New York: Random House, Inc., 2009.

The Willa Cather Archive
http://cather.unl.edu/life.longbio.html

The Willa Cather Foundation
http://www.willacather.org/about-willa-cather